The European Union Reform Treaty

How will it affect the UK?

John Palmer
and Peter Facey

January 2008

**Unlock
Democracy**
Charter88
New Politics Network

The European Union Reform Treaty: How Will it Affect the UK?
By John Palmer and Peter Facey
January 2008

Unlock Democracy argues and campaigns for a vibrant, inclusive democracy that puts power in the hands of the people.

The opinions expressed in this booklet reflect those of the individual authors only.

Published by
Unlock Democracy
6 Cynthia Street London N1 9JF

Phone +44 (0) 20 7278 4443
Fax +44 (0) 20 7278 4425
Email info@unlockdemocracy.org.uk

www.unlockdemocracy.org.uk

ISBN 978-0-9555523-3-5

Designed by SoapBox, www.soapboxcommunications.co.uk

Contents

Introduction

This booklet is a basic introduction to the European Union Reform Treaty, sometimes called the Lisbon Treaty. The first section of the booklet gives a brief guide to the key changes in the Treaty, and is written by John Palmer.

There is then a section by Peter Facey giving Unlock Democracy's views on whether the Treaty will help improve things in terms of representation, participation, rights, accountability, and transparency. This second section follows on from Charter 88's publication *Five Democratic Tests for Europe*. New Politics Network has been working for some years on the issue of citizen representation in Europe, partly through its Citizens in Europe project. Charter 88 and New Politics Network came together in 2006 to form Unlock Democracy. Thanks to everyone who helped with this project.

The European Union Reform Treaty – How Will it Affect the UK?

By John Palmer

Introduction

In recent years the pace and scope of what has become known as 'globalisation' has dominated political debate. While it has brought considerable economic advantages, globalisation has also created a degree of social dislocation and a sense of insecurity. Resentment at the impact of change on a once familiar economic and political environment has, for some, given way to a feeling that there are forces at work which seem beyond the control of democratic politicians.

For some citizens, the succession of European Union treaties in recent decades has fuelled this perception of a loss of democratic control over events. This, in turn, has created a difficult political climate in which to debate the merits of the new European Union Reform Treaty. **Ironically this treaty has been devised precisely to help the United Kingdom and the other EU Member States to bring globalisation under better management and regulation.** More than that, the Treaty, in part, aspires to make the EU a measure of quality for the future governance of globalisation – including the framework of rules, regulations, democratic accountability and legally enforceable rights within which globalisation should take place.

From the founding Treaty of Rome in 1957, the European Union has evolved over time through a series of treaties. These have laid the legal basis to allow Member States to act collectively on a range of challenges which governments have come to believe can better be met together, rather than by each country trying to act alone.

This guide seeks to explain what the Reform Treaty will mean in practice for citizens in the UK. It seeks to put into context the changes which are proposed to the way the EU institutions work and how EU Member States including the United Kingdom take decisions at the European level. It will look particularly at the likely impact of these changes on civil society and democratic politics.

The EU Reform Treaty was agreed by the heads of government of all 27 EU Member States at a summit meeting in Lisbon in October 2007. Only after all 27 have approved the new treaty can it enter into force. The planned target date for this is June 2009 when the next elections to the European Parliament will be held throughout the EU. This is also when decisions will have to be taken about the leadership and composition of the new European Commission, which has a five-year mandate. A clear understanding of the proposed new treaty will become even more important as the debate gets under way in the UK about its approval by Parliament.

How did the Reform Treaty come about?

By comparison with most other EU treaties since the 1957 Treaty of Rome, **the Reform Treaty is a modest affair indeed – a relatively small step where the Treaty of Rome was a giant leap forward.** It is sometimes forgotten that the Treaty of Rome – in its own words –

committed all participating states to work towards the goal of "an ever closer union among the European peoples." The most striking feature of the Treaty of Rome was the introduction of the principle of 'shared sovereignty.' This describes the way in which some decisions can be taken under supra-national EU law, rather than simply as a result of inter-governmental 'cooperation.' As we shall see later it was agreed at the outset of the European Union that – in defined areas – European law, as opposed to national law, would apply.

This was indeed a radical – even revolutionary – break with how relations between sovereign states were traditionally conducted. Sovereignty sharing was a response to the obvious limits and the sheer precariousness of mere 'cooperation' between potentially rival states. Over the centuries, the lack of binding relationships between European states helped create an environment which generated episodic crises and wars. It was a determination to break this destructive cycle that inspired the path breaking nature of EU 'shared' institutions and the wider project for European integration.

The Treaty of Rome established new supra-national institutions to function – as Member States decided – in limited and in clearly designated areas, under European law. In these areas European law would be held superior to national law. **The European Commission** was created to propose and administrate EU legislation. But national ministers from the Member State governments – meeting as the **Council of Ministers** – have always taken final decisions on whether or not to enact these laws.

An independent European Court of Justice was established to make binding judgements when there was legal conflict over decisions taken by EU institutions. The case law which has been developed over the past 50 years by the court has played an important part in the integration process.

The Treaty of Rome also provided for a **European Parliament** which, since 1979, has been directly elected by EU citizens in all Member States. Although it originally had only an 'advisory' role, today it shares law making powers in a growing number of areas with the Council of Ministers. These will increase further as a result of the Reform Treaty.

As the EU has enlarged from its original six Member States to 27 today, subsequent EU treaties – notably the Single European Act in 1986 and the Treaty of Maastricht in 1992 – further strengthened the decision making process at EU level. This was achieved by defining where specific decisions might be taken by governments through a **'Qualified Majority Vote'** rather than by unanimity. Under the Qualified Majority Vote system each country has an agreed number of votes in the Council of Ministers (depending on population size and other factors). A majority decision is achieved once a specified threshold of votes is reached.

Subsequent EU treaties also have defined **new 'common policy' areas.** For example the Single European Act created the 'border free' single European market to allow for the free movement of goods, capital, services and people across the EU. The Treaty of Maastricht authorised the introduction of the euro – the single currency now adopted by a majority of EU countries – although not the UK.

Some see in this series of EU treaties the workings of a hidden hand pushing the EU towards what is sometimes described as a 'federalist super state'. The 'federal' concept is long established in many European countries and is developing now in the UK as the different regions and nations within the British state (such as Scotland and Wales) exercise devolved power within agreed limits. In this model, the UK government itself is becoming a new British federal level authority in relation to the self-governing regions.

But the drive behind closer European integration has a more down to earth explanation. New governance arrangements for the European Union had to be agreed so the EU could deal with new (and sometimes unexpected) problems which Member States concluded they were unable to handle on their own. **The need to respond to these real world problems – rather than any ideological agenda in favour of European integration – has driven the development of the European Union.**

How was the Reform Treaty negotiated and agreed?

The traditional way of negotiating EU treaties always left a great deal to be desired. Treaty revision negotiations were traditionally hammered out 'behind closed doors' in meetings of ministers and officials from the Member State governments. Final agreement was reached in a special Inter-Governmental Conference (IGC) of ministerial representatives of the EU Member States. EU treaties have been put to public ratification – normally by a vote in national Member State parliaments. In only a very few cases have such decisions been taken by national referendum and in the case of the UK the only referendum was held in 1975 to approve accession to the EU – including agreement to the Treaty of Rome and other founding treaties and to confirm Wilson's renegotiation of the terms under which Britain had joined the EU in 1972.

In the case of the negotiations leading up to the Reform Treaty the process has been very different. As has been widely noted, the content of the Reform Treaty is very similar to the 'Treaty Establishing a European Union Constitution' which was agreed in 2004, but subsequently abandoned after being rejected in referendums in both France and the Netherlands.

The Constitutional Treaty was drafted as part of a long process of debate in a specially established Constitutional Convention, which produced the draft text. The Convention was composed not only of representatives of Member State governments and the EU institutions but also of elected members of both the European Parliament and national Member State parliaments. It met and debated in public and received testimony from a wide range of civil society organisations and interest groups from across the length and breadth of the Union.

This was another important break with the past. The 'Treaty Establishing a European Union Constitution' has now been abandoned, and the new Reform Treaty in practice consists only of a complex series of amendments to existing EU treaties. Thus the legal format of the Reform Treaty is different to the previous Constitutional Treaty. Moreover, it removes all symbols of a constitution. **But by retaining much of the content of the abandoned Constitutional Treaty, the Reform Treaty has harvested the output of the Convention process.**

What does the Reform Treaty do in practice?

The EU Reform Treaty amends existing Treaties in ways designed to help an EU of 27 Member States work more effectively. Governments believe approval of the Treaty will allow the EU to move on from debating institutional changes and focus on issues which matter to citizens: energy security, organised crime and terrorism, globalisation, further enlargement and making Europe's voice more effective internationally. Among the most important changes proposed are:

The creation of two new posts:

● **A long term President of the European Council,** appointed by national governments for a possible two terms of two and a half years each, replacing the current system where the Presidency of the European Council rotates every six months. The European Council is made up of the heads of state and government of Member States, holding summit meetings on average four times a year. (This should not be confused with the Council of Ministers, which describes the monthly meetings of national ministers on various policy areas). The European Council steers the political direction of the EU and takes the most important legislative decisions. The hope is that the European Council President will provide greater continuity in decision-making, as well as improve liaison and coordination between Member States in implementing agreed policies.

● **A High Representative of the European Union for Foreign Affairs and Security Policy** – who is likely to be better known as the new 'EU Foreign Minister'. He or she will be appointed by the European Council and with the agreement of the President of the European Commission. The High Representative will conduct the Union's Common Foreign and Security Policy (CFSP). In the words of the Amsterdam Treaty which established the CFSP its aims are:

- to safeguard the common values, fundamental interests, independence and integrity of the Union in conformity with the principle of the United Nations Charter;
- to strengthen the security of the Union in all ways;
- to preserve peace and strengthen international security, in accordance with the principles of the United Nations Charter, as well as the principle of the Helsinki Final Act and the objectives of the Paris Charter, including those on external borders;
- to promote international co-operation;
- to develop and consolidate democracy and the rule of law, and respect for human rights and fundamental freedoms.

Under the Reform Treaty Member States have agreed to give tasks to the High Representative on foreign policy and he or she will implement commonly agreed policies. The High Representative will merge two existing roles – that of the High Representative for the Common Foreign and Security Policy and the External Relations Commissioner. As Vice-President of the European Commission, he or she will be in charge of those aspects of EU external affairs – such as development aid – for which the Commission is responsible, as well as major foreign policy issues which remain the sole preserve of Member States' governments acting in cooperation. The creation of this new post should make the EU more coherent and effective in its dealings with the rest of the world.

- The High Representative will also be able to present agreed EU positions in international organisations – in the way that the Member State that holds the Presidency does now. The High Representative will be served by a European Action Service – seen by some as an embryo EU 'Diplomatic Service' – which will be drawn from serving Commission officials working on external policy and officials seconded from Member State foreign ministries. All CFSP policy decisions must be taken unanimously by all Member State governments. They can agree that some implementation decisions can be taken by a voting majority but this authorisation itself must be taken unanimously.

- **National parliaments will have a voice in influencing European laws for the first time.** Every national parliament will receive proposals for new EU legislation directly. They may judge whether the proposals conform to the principle of 'subsidiarity' (that the EU should only act where it adds value and does not replace or remove the rights of national or regional legislators). Moreover all EU decisions must be 'proportional' (that is, the actions of the EU should not be greater than is necessary to achieve the desired aims). If one third of national parliaments object, then the proposal will be sent back for review by the Commission (this is known as the 'yellow card'). If the Commission persists with its proposal with half of the national parliaments opposed, the Council of Ministers and the European Parliament must judge whether the Commission has violated its authority. However, when it comes to family law just one national parliament can veto the application of legislation in that Member State.

- **The numbers of Commissioners will be reduced** with the aim of creating a more efficient Commission. There is currently one Commissioner from each country in the EU (27 in all). From 2014, the number of Commissioners will be reduced, so only two-thirds of Member States provide a Commissioner at any time, with every country taking equal turns.

- **Qualified Majority Voting will be extended to 23 new and 26 existing policy areas.** These mostly deal with procedure rather than policy (for example, for the appointment of a High Representative for Foreign Affairs and Security Policy). But Qualified Majority Voting can be used in important areas of Justice and Policing (where the UK may decide not to 'opt in') as well as energy policy, humanitarian aid, and urgent financing of measures within the EU's Common Foreign and Security Policy. The Reform Treaty will also streamline and speed up decision-making in a number of technical areas such as appointments to the European Central Bank's executive board.

- Because the UK has insisted on maintaining a national veto in key areas of justice and home affairs, social security, tax, foreign policy and defence – overall – the impact on Britain of the extension of Qualified Majority Voting under the Reform Treaty will be significantly less than, for example, under the Single European Act or the Treaty of Maastricht. It should be noted that if the UK exercises the right to 'opt in' to decisions on Justice and Home affairs it will not be able to 'opt out' again. These special arrangements for the UK are sometimes referred to as the British government's 'red lines' which had to be respected for the UK to agree to the Reform Treaty.

- **A new, simpler mechanism has been devised for deciding what constitutes a "qualified majority" in the Council of Ministers.** This is designed to give a fairer weighting to Member States who previously believed they were under-represented in terms of their population size. Under the new 'Double Majority Voting' system, a minimum of 55% of the Member States (currently 15 out of 27 countries) representing a minimum of 65% of the EU's population must vote in favour for European legislation to be passed. The new system will start to come into force in 2014, with a transition period to 2017. The UK's share of votes in the Council of Ministers will increase.

- **The European Parliament will help decide EU legislation in 40 new policy areas.** This will give MEPs significant powers of law making (known as 'co-decision'), alongside national ministers in the Council of Ministers where decisions in future can be taken by Qualified Majority vote. For example, laws passed to tackle carbon emissions and climate change will now be taken jointly by the Council of Ministers representing Member State governments and the European Parliament.

- **The European Parliament will be able to elect the new President of the European Commission.** This opens the way for the pan-European political parties, which have been formed by like-minded national parties to fight elections to the European Parliament, to nominate their candidates for the post of European Commission President in the 2009 election. This would allow voters to effectively choose who will lead the most important of the EU supra-national executive bodies – the European Commission.

- **The rules governing 'enhanced co-operation'** where groups of EU countries may choose to integrate more closely with each other on certain issues – under an EU legal framework – **are simplified.** This protects the rights of countries which do not wish to participate. Under the Reform Treaty, at least a third of the Member States must want to co-operate, and others must be free to join at any time if they choose.

- **The Charter of Fundamental Rights is incorporated into EU law.** The Charter sets out in one place the rights which citizens across the EU already have, for example through the European Convention on Human Rights, or through existing EU law. Its aim is to ensure that EU institutions respect those fundamental rights. The Charter reaffirms existing rights and will apply to all Member States when they implement EU law. In other words the European Court of Justice can only make judgements when cases are brought against the EU institutions (European Commission, European Parliament, Council of Ministers). National courts will retain jurisdiction in cases involving domestic violations of the rights set out in the Charter.

● The Charter will not extend the powers of the European Union and the UK government has negotiated language in a protocol – a form of words added to the Treaty – to deny the right of the European Court to adjudicate on case law in ways which might affect UK legislation. The government says this arrangement will prevent the creation of any new social or economic rights other than those that are already provided in UK law. This has angered trade unionists and others concerned with issues of social justice in the UK. There may also be challenges to the UK protocol in cases where the European Court is obliged to take the provisions of the Charter into account in making case law. Under EU laws all rulings of the European Court of Justice should apply equally to all Member States.

Will the Treaty create a more effective EU?

The EU's ability to take effective and timely decisions has been obstructed and sometimes paralysed by the complexities of the existing decision making system. These problems have been compounded as the EU's membership has grown continuously in recent decades from the original six Member States to the present total of 27. Although enlargement of the EU cannot continue indefinitely, new members (notably from the western Balkans) will join over the next decade. The Reform Treaty is, on this view, the minimum needed if a still enlarging EU is to adapt policies to a fast-moving world. Thus:

- **The Reform Treaty should result in swifter and more consistent decisions** in immigration, security and cross-border crime – which forms part of the Freedom, Security and Justice strategy referred to above. When decisions in these areas are taken by qualified majority vote, a single state will no longer be able to veto the clear will of the great majority. This could mean an important enhancement of Europe's ability to combat terrorism, to tackle crime and human trafficking, and to manage migratory flows. However the UK has decided only to reserve the right to take part in these decisions and cannot be obliged to do so.

- **The European Union should have an improved ability to act in areas of major priority for EU citizens** such as energy policy, public health and civil protection. There are also new provisions to speed up decision making on climate change, public services, research and development, trade and commercial policy, humanitarian aid, sport, and tourism.

- **The simplified way of calculating qualified majority voting should strengthen the efficiency of the EU Council of Ministers** and provide a clearer balance between the number of Member States and the size of the population needed for a 'Qualified Majority.'

- When some governments are reluctant to implement a new policy a group of **at least nine Member States may take collective action inside the EU framework under the 'enhanced cooperation' procedures.** This could open the way for groups of countries to integrate more ambitiously with each other in areas where cross-border action can lead to more effective results – for instance in judicial cooperation in criminal matters and police cooperation.

- **The President of the European Council should help ensure there is better preparation and continuity in the work of the Heads of Government.** A streamlined Commission, with reinforced authority for its President, should help the EU focus on the wider European interest.

- **The new High Representative for Foreign and Security Policy/Vice** President of the Commission for External Affairs and the creation of the European External Action Service (an embryo EU diplomatic service) should make a **clear difference to the EU's capacity to tackle global problems.**

- **The new treaty will give the EU a 'legal personality'** which should facilitate its capacity to sign international agreements.

Will the Reform Treaty do the job?

Some critics of the European Union will, naturally, oppose any treaty which seeks to give it greater coherence and effectiveness. But there are also those who will regret the modesty of the new treaty and its failure to tackle some of the most important defects in the present governance arrangements of the EU.

- **All significant decisions in the fields of foreign, security, defence policy as well as important areas of economic coordination policy (notably fiscal policy) remain subject to the national veto.** This will not make it easier to agree common policies in these areas. This unanimity requirement will also complicate steps to agree how, for example, the European Union should be represented in global organisations – such as the United Nations or the international financial institutions (International Monetary Fund, World Bank) which – most agree – should be reformed and made more representative.

- **All future institutional reforms may still be subject to the national veto.** This will make it difficult for the European Union to adapt to circumstances that may warrant further changes to the way it functions. However there will be an opportunity to review how the system is functioning every time a new treaty linked to the accession of a new Member State has to be approved by the existing 27 countries.

- **Uncertainty surrounds the practical arrangements governing how the President of the European Council, the EU 'Foreign Minister' and the future Presidents of the Commission will work together.** Matters may be further complicated because 'teams' of three Member States will still rotate among themselves to take responsibility for running the business of the Council of Ministers, except foreign policy where this will be the responsibility of the new High Representative. These issues and the question of who will represent the EU at major international meetings remains unclear and will have to be resolved by future decisions of the Council of Ministers before the Treaty comes into force.

- Since economic reform and innovation will remain subject to the national veto it remains to be seen how effective the Union will be in implementing its sometimes ambitious targets to become the most competitive, most innovative, most socially cohesive and environmentally sustainable economy in the world.

Will the EU become more democratic and transparent?

Supporters of the Reform Treaty claim that it will refresh and reinforce the European Union's democratic infrastructure. They say it should result in more open institutions and greater opportunities for Europeans to have their voice heard in the work of the EU. A new section of the Treaty lays out the principles underlying the European Union's democratic accountability which will allow citizens to better understand how the system works and in what ways it is accountable.

- The increase of law making by 'co-decision' (in around 40 areas) means that the elected European Parliament will be placed on an equal footing with the EU Council of Ministers for the vast bulk of EU legislation. This will include key issues under the umbrella of 'Freedom, Security and Justice'. The Parliament will also see important new powers over the EU budget and international agreements entered into by the EU.

- The new rights for national parliaments offer a valuable opportunity for them to become more involved in the work of the EU while respecting the established roles of the EU institutions. Whether they exploit these new opportunities to play a more effective role remains to be seen. Some national parliaments already involve expert members of the European Parliament as non-voting members of scrutiny committees which subject draft EU laws to close examination where their implementation requires parliamentary approval. But national parliaments will also have to develop a more effective network with each other to be able to mobilise the support needed to force a reconsideration of Commission proposals.

● **Opening up the legislative discussions in the Council of Ministers to the public will enable citizens and national parliaments to see the decisions taken by their governments** at first hand. It remains to be seen whether full advantage of these provisions will be taken up both by the media and representatives of civil society organisations and national parliaments.

● **The new right of 'Citizens' Initiative'** will make it possible for a million citizens from different Member States – out of the Union's population of almost 500 million – to trigger an invitation to the European Commission to bring forward a new proposal. This innovation should encourage non-governmental organisations and similar bodies to monitor developments at EU level more closely and ensure effective working partnerships with similar organisations in other Member States in pursuing these initiatives.

● **The complex relationship between the Member States and the European Union should become more obvious** with the clear categorisation of the competences (or powers) of both the EU institutions and national (and regional) authorities in Member States.

● **The recognition in the Reform Treaty that Member States remain inside the Union only if they so choose,** with a provision recognising that withdrawal from the EU is an option, **should help allay fears** that Member States have lost any right to withdraw.

Democracy in the EU – what more should be done?

In spite of these steps forward, progress towards a more democratic and transparent Union remains limited. The Reform Treaty itself – consisting of complex amendments to existing articles in other EU treaties – is less user friendly than the ill-fated Constitutional Treaty.

Moreover:

- **Debate in Britain has focussed on the government's decision to ratify the treaty through a vote in Parliament rather than by referendum.** A number of EU Member States did organise referendums to ratify the Constitutional Treaty (there were two "Yes" decisions in Portugal and Luxembourg as well as the "No" votes in France and the Netherlands). But in Germany the possibility of holding referendums is excluded by the national constitution – something which was pressed on the German people by the victorious allied powers after the second world war.

- **Although the European Parliament has won more 'co-decision' powers, with the Council of Ministers, in passing law, they have virtually no role in very important areas decided by inter-governmental cooperation.** In foreign policy, taxation and broad macro-economic policy the elected MEPs can only exploit their rights to be consulted to the maximum. This underlines the importance of a much closer liaison between European and national parliamentarians (and, where appropriate) members of regional

parliaments to ensure effective scrutiny of the actions of governments.

● **Some may also question whether the European Commission
should retain the sole right to propose legislation to the Council of
Ministers. In the past this monopoly has been justified by the fact
that only the Commission was responsible** for the collective
European interest and not just national interests. But given a de facto
(but healthy) politicisation emerging in the Commission there may be
a case for that right of initiative to be shared with the European
Parliament. More also needs to be done to improve citizens' access
to information at EU level. But it is important to recognise the
enormous strides taken in recent years particularly by the European
Commission. The Council of Ministers – under pressure from national
governments – tends to be less open. But the biggest area of
concern where the lack of transparency affects civil liberties is
precisely in areas of policy where decisions are taken by inter-
governmental cooperation and not under European Union law. This
is particularly worrying in the new areas of security cooperation
between Member States dealing with cross border crime and
terrorism.

Involving citizens with the EU

It would be foolish to pretend that even after this treaty comes into
force there will not still be a worrying gulf in public understanding of and
involvement in the activity of the European Union. Improved EU
information and communications can help but to be effective there
should be shared ownership with the EU institutions for the messages
delivered to the public. In other words where key messages and

communications are going out in the name of the European Union they should be agreed jointly by the EU institutions and national governments. Too often at present contradictory messages are given.

The current democratic problem has deeper roots than in poor or inconsistent information and communication. There is a widespread view that EU decision-makers (especially governments acting together in the Council of Ministers) are not being held properly to account. Voters are confused about the division of responsibilities between regional, national and European levels of governance. They have no clear understanding of who is responsible for what – and who is accountable to whom – within the decision-making architecture. Moreover European citizens today expect not only to be informed but also to be consulted about the future direction of decision-making bodies.

The European Citizens' Consultations (http://www.european-citizens-consultations.eu) launched by non-party political, not-for-profit foundations and a range of other organisations, to develop radical new ways of consulting citizens on European issues, have a part to play. They provide an opportunity for members of the public from all 27 Member States to debate the future of the EU across the boundaries of geography and language. The aim is to establish a model for European citizens' participation in the future using a range of innovative techniques.

However the most important way to ensure citizens' ownership of the European Union political process – especially since it is now becoming more politicised – will be if European political parties offer serious alternatives to voters about the direction the EU should take. A first step would be for the parties to fight the 2009 European

Parliament elections not only with concrete and clearly varying political programmes for the EU – but also offering voters a choice on who the Parliament should elect to lead the European Commission.

Is this the last treaty or will there be more to come?

Most EU governments insist that the adoption of the Reform Treaty should mean that there will be no further debate about reforming the EU institutions for some years to come. The priority for the coming decade is likely to be policy, and policy implementation. It is always difficult to predict what the new policy challenges will be. A few years ago few would have forecast that action to deal with climate change – and in particular carbon emissions – would be so urgent. But now many of these decisions are to be taken through the EU legal process. Some predict a similar development in energy policy – both energy security and energy infrastructure.

As the EU and its Member States engage at an ever deeper level with the new global challenges and threats, the need to further strengthen the Common Foreign, Security and Defence Policy would not be surprising. However the timing of any action to take European integration further – beyond the steps agreed in the Reform Treaty – is likely to be linked to the next (possibly final) stage of European Union enlargement.

Around 2015 decisions will probably have to be taken about whether or not to admit Turkey, Albania and the republics of the former Yugoslavia (apart from Slovenia which is already a member). This will encourage debate over the final size and shape of the European

Union and its role in an ever more inter-dependent world. It is inevitable that the way the EU governs itself will become part of that debate.

The question is whether civil society and democratic organisations in the UK and the other Member States will be better placed to influence the debate and the decisions which may result. For this to happen, a clearer understanding of how the European Union functions and what challenges it faces now and in the future is essential.

John Palmer was the Brussels-based European Editor of *The Guardian* between 1975 and 1997. He was the Founding Political Director of the *European Policy Centre* in Brussels for ten years and is now a member of its Advisory Council. He is also a member of the EU Advisory Council of *TASC (Think Tank for Action on Social Change)*, Dublin, a member of the Advisory Board of the *Federal Trust*, London. He is a Visiting (Practitioner) Fellow with the *European Institute, the University of Sussex*, UK and a member of the Advisory Group of the *Globus et Locus Governance of Globalisation Network*, Milan.

Books published: *Europe Without America – the crisis in Atlantic relations* (Oxford University Press 1987); *Trading Places – the future of the European Community* (Hutchinson's, London 1989); *1992 and beyond – the European Community into the 21st Century* (The European Commission, Brussels 1991).

Unlock Democracy's Five Tests for the EU Reform Treaty

By Peter Facey

Introduction

In 2003, Charter 88 published *Five Democratic Tests for Europe*, which measured the government of the European Union against five key democratic standards. Related to this Treaty, these are:

- **Representation:** does the Treaty improve the representation of citizens in the European Union?
- **Participation:** does the Treaty increase the opportunities for EU citizens to participate in EU affairs?
- **Rights:** does the Treaty ensure that the rights of EU citizens and member states are safeguarded?
- **Accountability:** does the Treaty improve the accountability of EU institutions?
- **Openness and transparency:** does the Treaty improve the openness and transparency of European Union institutions?

We have used the tests to judge whether the EU Reform Treaty would improve the quality of democracy at the European Union level.

As an organisation we are neutral on whether the UK should be a member of the European Union (EU) – our view is simply that if we are, the European Union should be as democratic and transparent as possible. In this publication we don't comment on what would be the ideal form of government in the EU, if any. We only give our views on whether some of the specific measures proposed by the Treaty meet our five tests.

1. Representation

Under the Treaty, national parliaments would have eight weeks to look at legislation proposed by the EU. This 'yellow card' system means that if one third of Member States object, the Commission (which proposes legislation) would have to review the draft, and give reasons for then deciding whether or how to proceed with it. This should provide better coordination between national parliaments and the Union and provide a further check on the EU taking decisions on areas that are better decided at national or local level.

The eventual introduction of Double Majority Voting, whereby decisions that are not taken by unanimity will need to have the support of 55% of Member States and 65% of the population of the Union, will ensure greater transparency and ensure that there is a fairer balance between big and small states. In addition, if either 75% of Member States or Member States representing 75% of the population indicate that they oppose a proposal, the Council will delay adoption in favour of extending discussion in the hope of reaching a mutually satisfactory solution.

The European Parliament will get an equal say over legislation with the Council in about 40 new areas, so called co-decision. This will have the effect of strengthening the elected Parliament and in effect give the Union greater democratic legitimacy. The Treaty also sees the UK gain an extra MEP.

Members of the European Commission do not represent their Member States as such, but have the role of identifying and representing the common European interest. In practice, of course, Commissioners cannot escape the political culture of the Member States from which they come. A reduction in the number of Commissioners, desirable for reasons of efficiency, therefore needs to be accompanied by deliberate measures to ensure that the breadth of representation is still maintained.

2. Participation

The Treaty provides that treaties can in some instances be amended without needing to have a full intergovernmental conference. They would still need to be agreed unanimously and have the approval of all national parliaments. This would leave intergovernmental conferences in future for major reforms to the treaties and in these circumstances we would support a referendum in the UK.

The Treaty gives a right for citizens to request that the Commission consider legislation – if at least one million EU citizens ask for it. This is known as a 'citizens' initiative'. This is a positive development which will hopefully increase meaningful participation by citizens and civil society groups.

3. Rights

The Charter of Fundamental Rights will have "the same legal value as the Treaties", but there is a protocol attached to it, which says that the Charter does not create any new rights for those in the UK, and that no court will get any new rights to strike down UK law. There has been some debate over whether this will be the case in practice. Regardless of the opt-out, all EU law will be subject to the Charter and so in practice UK citizens will be subject to most laws that are subject to it in any case. What the opt-out does mean however is that UK citizens, unlike the citizens of other Member States, will not be able to bring a case to the European Court of Justice on the grounds that European law has infringed their rights. This appears to be the worst of all worlds: UK citizens will still be subject to laws made under the Charter but will have no means for redress.

Article 3b of the Treaty explicitly states that: "Under the principle of conferral, the Union shall act only within the limits of the competences conferred upon it by the Member States in the Treaties to attain the objectives set out therein. Competences not conferred upon the Union in the Treaties remain with the Member States." Coupled with the fact that the Treaty can only be amended by unanimity, this is a guarantee of the rights of the Member States.

Furthermore, the Treaty includes a clause that for the first time gives Member States the explicit right to leave the Union. While this right has always been implicit under international law anyway, it is in effect a recognition that Member States are sovereign and that while they may agree to pool sovereignty, that sovereignty ultimately lies with the Member States and their citizens. Far from the creation of an EU "superstate", the Reform Treaty explicitly rules this out.

4. Accountability

The current EU Presidency, which lasts six months and is held by a Member State, will be replaced with a new post of President of the

European Council. This President will be an individual, with a term lasting 2.5 years and will be appointed by the Council, not the Parliament. This may result in greater accountability due to being able to track actions of an individual over a longer period of time, though this is not certain.

The nomination of president of the European Commission will be made "Taking into account the elections to the European Parliament" (article 9d), and that candidate shall be "elected by the European Parliament by a majority of its component members." This opens up the possibility that the Commission president will have the same kind of accountability as currently enjoyed by prime ministers in national governments.

For those citizens who are concerned about the way in which the EU exercises (or does not exercise) a role on the world stage, the creation of the post of High Representative of the Union for Foreign Affairs and Security Policy will be a welcome increase in accountability. The different roles of the Commission and the Council of Ministers will be better coordinated and the EU's voice on common issues will be clearer. The decision-making method for foreign policy remains essentially unchanged – unanimity for policy positions, majority voting for their implementation – which means that Member State foreign ministers remain in charge of foreign policies where they choose to do so: an increase in EU accountability is not at the expense of national accountability.

5. Openness and transparency

The Council of Ministers, under the Treaty, is committed to meeting in public when dealing with legislation. This is a significant increase in transparency.

The Treaty gives the EU its own legal personality, and it is confirmed in a Declaration which is not legally binding that it can only act where Member States have actually transferred areas of power (also called 'competences') to it.

However, the process of negotiating this Treaty has not been transparent enough – much of the negotiation happened behind closed doors and in a tight timeframe which has made it difficult for the UK Parliament to participate in the process. The Treaty itself is extremely difficult to read as it consists largely of amendments to the previous treaties, so it has been very difficult for UK citizens to read and judge it for themselves.

Conclusion

The European Union is based on the idea of Member States pooling their sovereignty to be able to tackle common problems.

For many critics of the European Union it is this very pooling – or as they would argue, ceding – of sovereignty that is the problem. If you take this position, then the Reform Treaty does little to address your concerns. In fact as it increases the power of the Union with a limited extension of majority voting, reduction in national vetoes and an increase in competence then it will be regarded as negative step.

With that said, the EU is gaining far fewer powers in this treaty than it did under the Single European Act or the Maastricht Treaty. Indeed, the explicit recognition of Member States' autonomy and even the laying out of a procedure for leaving the European Union make it clear that the idea of a European "federal superstate" is completely off the agenda.

By contrast, if you are more concerned about the nature of democracy rather than national sovereignty then the Reform Treaty offers some real improvements. It increases the role of the directly elected European Parliament, increases the powers of national parliaments, improves the openness and transparency of the Council of Ministers and gives citizens a right of initiative to raise issues directly with the European Commission. These are all significant steps forward.

It isn't all good news however. The 'opt-out' secured by the UK government on the Charter of Fundamental Rights is highly problematic and will mean that while UK citizens will remain subject to European law made under the Charter they will lack the same rights that other European citizens will have to seek redress if European laws infringe on their rights. This would appear to be the worst of all possible options. This, however, is a criticism of the UK's opt out, not the principle of having a Charter of Fundamental Rights, which we support.

The Treaty's very complexity is also a backwards step. Its unreadability is bad for democracy as it effectively hands significant powers to judges and lawyers who will be the ultimate arbitrators over what it says. Spelling out all the powers and functions of the European Union in a single document which superseded all the previous treaties would have been a far better step. It is a great shame that such a single document was not politically feasible.

Our recent report, *British Citizens and the European Union* (Unlock Democracy, 2007) suggested that it was concerns about democracy and fairness, not national sovereignty, that most exercised British citizens about the EU. On balance therefore, we welcome the Reform Treaty as a step forward.

Unlock Democracy believes that a referendum should be held for all major treaty changes and this is no exception. We are however mindful of the fact that some previous treaties were far more significant than this one. With that in mind, we are open to the suggestion that a referendum on membership itself would be more appropriate at this stage. Any national debate on the Reform Treaty is bound to become a debate about membership by extension in any case.

Finally, the UK government could and should do much more in terms of providing the British public with balanced information about how the EU works and increasing the scrutiny role of the UK Parliament over what ministers negotiate at the Council of the European Union. Ultimately, many of the problems associated with the EU and democracy are rooted in the undemocratic nature of UK governance itself. Until we have a stronger, more representative and more accountable Parliament, British citizens' interests will always be poorly served at an EU level.

Peter Facey is the Director of Unlock Democracy. He became the Director of Unlock Democracy's predecessor organisation the New Politics Network in July 2001. He later became director of Charter 88. He has worked in democratic reform and participation for 12 years and was previously Chief Executive for the British Youth Council. As Parliamentary and Press Officer for the Electoral Reform Society, he worked on the Jenkins Commission on Electoral Reform and the introduction of proportional representation for the European Parliament.

Further information on the Treaty

This booklet can only provide limited information on the Treaty and the European Union in general. Here are some suggestions for other places you might want to find a range of information on these subjects:

Government and Parliamentary information
The Foreign and Commonwealth Office – this government department has a website dedicated to the UK's relationship with the EU, and the reform treaty in particular. It is at: www.fco.gov.uk, then follow the links to 'Britain in the EU'. You can call the FCO at 020 7008 1500.

Discussions in Parliament can be a useful way of getting more information – see the Westminster Parliament's website at www.parliament.uk for example.

The House of Commons Library produced a useful briefing on the treaty in the weeks before it was signed – you can find this online at: http://www.parliament.uk/commons/lib/research/rp2007/rp07-080.pdf

Civil Society information
Centre for European Reform – a pro-Europe group. Their website is at: www.cer.org.uk. 14 Great College Street, London SW1P 3RX.
Tel: 020 7233 1199.

Open Europe – a group arguing for radical reform of the EU. Their website is at www.openeurope.org.uk. 7 Tufton Street, London, SW1P 3QN, Tel: 020 7197 2333.

Media information

Most newspapers have written pieces about the treaty, and about the EU more generally. You can search their websites for more information, as well as reading the papers or watching the television news.

Some useful websites are:

www.bbc.co.uk,
www.guardian.co.uk,
www.telegraph.co.uk.

Further Reading:

Five Democratic Tests for Europe (Charter 88, 2003)
A Europe for Citizens (New Politics Network, 2005)
British Citizens and the European Union (Unlock Democracy, 2007)

All are available to download for free from the Unlock Democracy website (www.unlockdemocracy.org.uk).

Glossary of terms

This glossary is a shorter edited version of that produced by the National Forum on Europe in Ireland, in its publication *Summary of the European Constitution* and is reproduced here with permission and thanks.

Accountability
The capacity or duty to account in an open, transparent manner for actions taken, or not taken, whether by an individual or an institution.

Charter of Fundamental Rights
This Charter, first drafted and adopted by an earlier Convention in October 2000, sets out in a single text, for the first time in the European Union's history, the civil, political, economic and social rights and freedoms of European citizens and all persons resident in the EU. It will come into force in the Reform Treaty, although a special 'opt-out' means that it will not apply in cases in the UK courts.

Co-decision
The procedure through which the Council of Ministers and the European Parliament enact much EU legislation: both bodies have to agree before a law can be passed. The Reform Treaty will apply this procedure to almost all legislation and also to the EU budget.

Common Foreign and Security Policy (CFSP)
The Common Foreign and Security Policy was established within the European Union in the 1992 Treaty on European Union, signed

at Maastricht. The common policy exists in addition to the separate foreign and security policies of the EU Member States. A number of important changes were introduced in the Amsterdam Treaty, which came into force in 1999, and since then there have been numerous developments in Common Foreign and Security Policy, including under the Nice Treaty.

The common policy is concerned with foreign affairs of a political character where the Member States judge that the broad objectives they share can more effectively be achieved by acting together or by coordinating their actions rather than by acting separately or in an uncoordinated fashion.

Conferral
This is the principle whereby the EU has only the powers conferred on its institutions by the treaties. Powers not conferred remain with the Member States.

Constitution
The body of fundamental principles or established precedents according to which a state or other organisation is governed— usually, but not always, set out in writing in a series of articles contained in a basic document.

Council of Europe
The Council of Europe is an intergovernmental organisation, set up in 1948, which includes in its aims the protection of human rights and the promotion and awareness of Europe's cultural identity and diversity. It has a wider membership than the EU. Though all Member States of the EU are also members of the Council of Europe, the latter is a distinct organisation in its own right.

Council of Ministers (properly called just the Council)

The Council of Ministers is the EU institution in which the governments of the Member States are represented. The Council consists of one representative of each Member State at Ministerial level. The Council meets in a whole range of formations, mainly sectoral (e.g. the Ministers for Agriculture when the Council takes decisions on the Common Agricultural Policy). The President (or chair) of the Council is the Minister of the Member State currently holding the Presidency of the EU. The High Representative is to chair the Foreign Affairs Council. Up to now, this was for a six-month term according to an agreed and equal rotation. (http://www.consilium.europa.eu/cms3_fo/showPage.asp?lang=EN).

European Commission

The European Commission is one of the EU institutions, representing the European interest common to all Member States. The Commission is the driving force in the legislative process, proposing the legislation on which the European Parliament and the Council of Ministers make decisions. Members of the Commission swear an oath of independence, distancing themselves from partisan influence from any source. Under the Reform Treaty, the number of members of the European Commission will be reduced from 27 (1 per Member State) to 18. (http://europa.eu.int/comm/index_en.htm).

European Council

The European Council is the EU institution representing the Heads of State or Government of the Member States. It meets typically four times a year and its functions are to define general policy guidelines and priorities for the EU and resolve the most difficult issues. Under the Reform Treaty, it will have a permanent president, in place of the rotating chairmanship that exists at present.

European Convention on Human Rights (ECHR)

The European Convention on Human Rights and Fundamental Freedoms, signed in 1950 under the aegis of the Council of Europe, sets out a list of human rights, which the participating countries guarantee to respect and uphold. The Convention established, for the first time, a system of international protection for human rights offering individuals the possibility of applying to a dedicated international court—the European Court of Human Rights—for the enforcement of their rights. All Member States of the Union have ratified the Convention.

European Court of Justice

This is the institution responsible for interpreting and enforcing Community law. The Court has one judge from each Member State. It has jurisdiction in disputes between Member States, between the Union and its Member States and between institutions and private individuals and the Union about matters that fall within the remit of the EU or are regulated by EU legislation or decisions. (http://curia.eu.int/en/index.htm).

European Parliament

The European Parliament is the EU institution that represents the citizens of the Member States. Under the Reform Treaty, it will have a maximum of 750 members, directly elected by the electorates in the 27 Member States. In many areas, the Parliament acts as co-legislator with the Council of Ministers. (http://www.europarl.eu.int).

European Security and Defence Policy (ESDP)

Established in 1999 at the Cologne European Council, the ESDP aims to allow the Union to develop its civilian and military capacities for crisis management and conflict prevention at international level, thus helping to maintain peace and international security, in accordance with the United Nations Charter.

Geneva Convention
UN rules on asylum dating from 1951. They give every refugee the right to have an application for asylum at least considered by the country in which they apply.

Harmonisation
This means co-ordinating national policies, rules and technical standards so closely that goods, services, capital and labour can move freely throughout the EU.

Intergovernmental
Describing institutions which cover more than one country and which are controlled entirely by national governments. In the EU, this refers principally to the Council of Ministers and the European Council. It is the opposite of supranational.

Intergovernmental Conference (IGC)
This is the term used to describe negotiations between the governments of the Member States through which amendments to the EU treaties are agreed.

Legal Personality
Under the Reform Treaty, the EU will acquire legal personality which means that it will be able to conclude international treaties or accede to agreements or conventions that have binding legal force. It will only be able to do so with the approval of the Member States.

Protocol
A protocol is a legal text annexed to a treaty which deals in a more detailed way with a certain topic. In the Reform Treaty, for example, there is a protocol on subsidiarity and the role of national parliaments. A

protocol to a treaty has the same legal status as the treaty itself when it has been ratified by the Member States.

Qualified Majority Voting (QMV)
QMV is the form of decision-making usually used in the Council of Ministers. Under the Reform Treaty, a vote to be passed will need the support of Member States representing 55% of the number of Member States and 65% of the population. This is intended to balance the interest of both large Member States and small ones.

Ratification
This is the process by which each individual Member State formally decides, through its own national procedures, that the Treaty should be legally binding on them. All Member States must ratify EU treaties in order for them to come into force.

Reasoned Opinion
The European Commission scrutinises steps taken by each Member State to implement EU law and, if dissatisfied, may issue a "reasoned opinion" outlining the measures that will need to be taken in order for the Member State to fully implement the EU law in question. Should these measures not be taken, then the Commission refers the matter to the European Court of Justice.

A second meaning of the term arises in the protocol to the Reform Treaty on applying the principles of subsidiarity and proportionality. There, the term refers to an opinion with reasons, put forward by a national parliament or a chamber thereof, that a proposal for a law, made by the Commission, is in breach of one of these two principles.

Subsidiarity
The principle whereby action is only taken by the European Union if it cannot be taken effectively at national level.